Ethereum:

Best Strategies for Investing and

Profiting From Ethereum

MARK CLARKSON

Table of Contents

Introduction

Congratulations on purchasing this book and thank you for doing so.

Unless you've been living with your head underground, you've heard a lot about cryptocurrencies in the past year. Terms like Blockchain and Bitcoin have literally become household words. For those who are interested in tapping into this market to create their own fortune, it can be a thrilling experience. Investing in cryptocurrencies now can be likened to investing in the automobile after Ford invented the horseless carriage. You're getting in on the ground floor of something you know will change the world.

But in this new and exciting digital world, there are lots of cryptocurrency networks that have the potential to lead an investor to a lot of money, each with their own unique characteristics. Ethereum is one of them, a currency that is expected to change the world's view on more than just an economic level.

It is Ethereum's unique qualities that are slowly changing the way we think about data and how to share it, utilize it, and protect it. Anyone interested in investing in it must first come to understand the complex infrastructure that surrounds it, the qualities that separate it from all other investment opportunities. As you grow in knowledge about these things, you'll begin to grasp why Ethereum could change the way the world does business on many levels.

It is that uniqueness that has seen it grow exponentially in a very short period of time. We've witnessed phenomenal growth with increases that went more than 4,000% without any sign of slowing. Where else will you find a profit potential like this? It is this kind of growth that has peaked the interest of people all over the globe. Even those who had no previous inclination to invest in any form are now wondering exactly what Ethereum is and how they can tap into this highly lucrative market.

Regardless of where you live, launching an investment career with Ethereum will first require you to change your mindset about currency in many ways. In fact, once you learn more about it, you'll quickly realize that you won't even be able to look at it in the same way you would with any other cryptocurrency.

Before Ethereum was developed, the Blockchain was only being used as a form of currency exchange. With the introduction of Bitcoin, the Blockchain allowed a peer-to-peer transfer of monetary assets that cut out the need for third party involvement. This was all done through a combination of complex codes and the application of complicated algorithms.

The developer of Ethereum saw immense potential with this new type of technology that went far beyond the transfer of funds. He saw that by adding another level of coding, it was possible to place many other types of data using the same Blockchain Technology. His concept is what paved the way for Ethereum.

Today, Ethereum is the number two cryptocurrency on the market and has used the Blockchain in a countless number of ways. Because of that, all sorts of people are now looking at Ethereum and trying to determine just how they can utilize this highly practical asset in their line of business.

In this book, we plan to point out how you can take advantage of those differences and use them as a means of growing your own investment income. In the following chapters we plan to discuss:

- What Ethereum actually is and why it is so different.

- How it was created

- How it works

- Investment Strategies for Ethereum

- How to Trade Ethereum

- How to make use of the tools located on the exchanges

As the second largest coin in the cryptocurrency market, Ethereum has already had a huge impact on the world economic scene. Analysts predict that very soon, it will extend its reaches even further into the business world. With implications that it will one day have an even wider scope is inevitable. This opens the door to immeasurable profit potential that extends far beyond what you might expect.

So, if you are ready to tap into an investment resource that defies the current way of doing business, if you're prepared to step out of the realm of our present economic structure, and you're brave enough to venture into a completely new way of making money, then you're ready to join many others who have found a huge potential for profit in doing something that is completely out of the norm. If that's you, then let's get started.

There are plenty of books on this subject on the market, thanks again for choosing this one! Every effort was made to ensure it is full of as much useful information as possible, please enjoy!

Chapter 1: What is Ethereum

To understand how Ethereum works you first need to understand Blockchain Technology and how it works. Since it is our old system of currency that sparked the impetus to change for something better, the more we understand the challenges and complexities of it the more we will appreciate what this new technology can do. Without the flaws in our traditional methods of exchanging value, the idea for the Blockchain and cryptocurrency may not have appeared for many more years.

Life Before the Blockchain

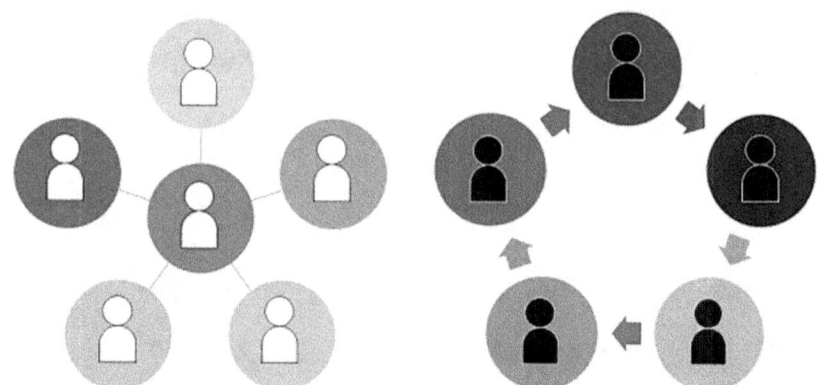

CENTRALIZATION VS DECENTRALIZATION

Before any of us had any idea of what a Blockchain or cryptocurrency was, practically everything we did was done with the aid of centralized networks. When you were issued your first social security card, when you got your driver's license, your school transcripts, and even your medical records, it was all stored on a centralized server.

Maintaining data on centralized servers was the only way anything was done. So, when you opened up your first bank account, you went to your bank, gave them your personal identification, handed them over your money to make a deposit and trusted that they would protect your identity and your money. The bank then took all the information you gave them, wrote it all down in a single ledger, which was kept along with everyone else's information on a single computer server.

For years, no one could access their money, health records, school documents, public history, or credit history without the aid of a middleman to retrieve it from that server. This third party usually charged us some pretty hefty fees to connect us to our own possessions. Financial institutions were the best at monopolizing these centralized servers, which were basically just a single computer they had total control over.

Many of us just accepted this arrangement because we had no other choice; there were no other alternatives to assist us in managing our money. But over time, we came to realize that a centralized server was not always serving in the best interest of the user. The middleman discovered that he wielded an incredible amount of power and eventually it became obvious that others had easier access to our data than we did. Banks could freeze our accounts without warning, our money was lent out to others without our consent, and our accounts could be closed without our knowledge, but we accepted these things because we knew there was nothing we could do about it; at least until Blockchain Technology came about.

What is Blockchain Technology?

To put it simply, Blockchain Technology is the ability to remove data from a single server, encrypt it with complex codes, and place it on a public ledger that is distributed to thousands of computers around the globe. Now, the information is not under the control of a single entity but is easily accessible to the authorized parties. While the data can be accessed from any computer, the ability to decrypt it lies in the hands of the owner, the only person that holds the keys to decipher the complex codes.

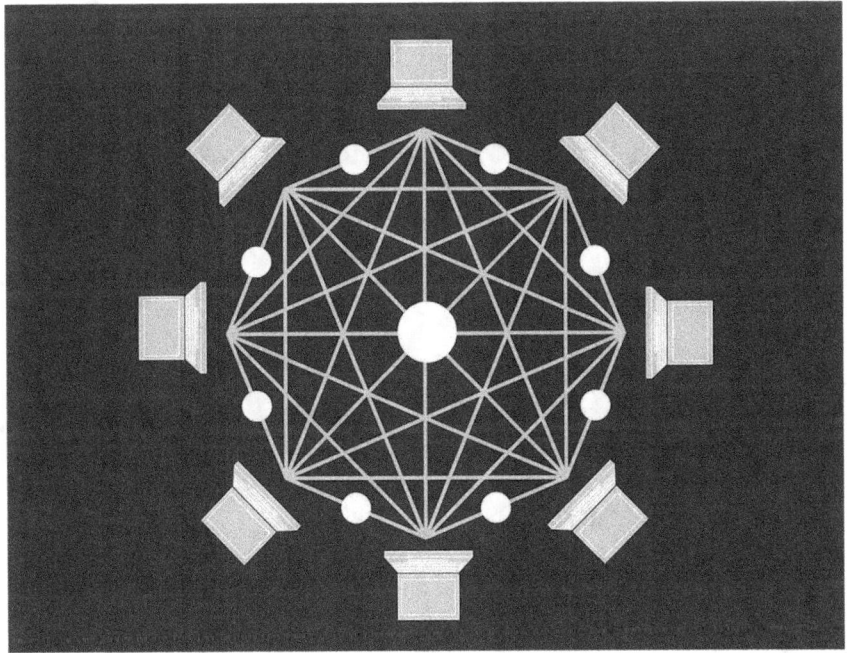

On the surface, this may not seem like a very big change. One still has to access the Internet to claim their data and access their own possessions. This new technology, however, meant that no third party had the power to dictate to the owner of the data what they could do with it. Users now could send funds to anyone they choose to without having to go through a huge and insensitive financial institution. It meant they could save on exorbitant fees, and it meant that they now had total control of their financial power.

Bitcoin opened the door for peer-to-peer transactions on a whole new level. However, once introduced, it was not long before others discovered that they could adapt it to other aspects of the digital world. With Bitcoin, users could not only send currency to their peers but across borders without having to pay hefty fees in the process.

How Does the Blockchain Work?

The basic concept of the Blockchain is pretty straightforward. It does the exact opposite of working with a centralized server. Once the data is uploaded into the system, it is encrypted, copied, verified, and then distributed to thousands of computers connected to the network. This way, the data is not saved on a single computer with an impersonal guard blocking access and charging tolls, but it exists everywhere within the network.

The benefits of this are obvious. Aside from the user having full control over what happens to his money, the system is free from most of the vulnerabilities that our older system had like the threat of hacking by identity and cyber thieves, viruses, and malware. Users now could store their money any way they wanted, access it whenever they choose and distribute it to whomever they please without having to include anyone else in the transaction. No threat could compromise the system since an issue with one computer cannot infect all the others in the network. As a result, the user's privacy could remain completely intact.

By design, the system is almost foolproof. By being distributed to thousands of computers throughout the network, there is no single point where the system can be compromised. If one computer goes down, there are thousands of others where the data can be retrieved with no break in the flow of transactions.

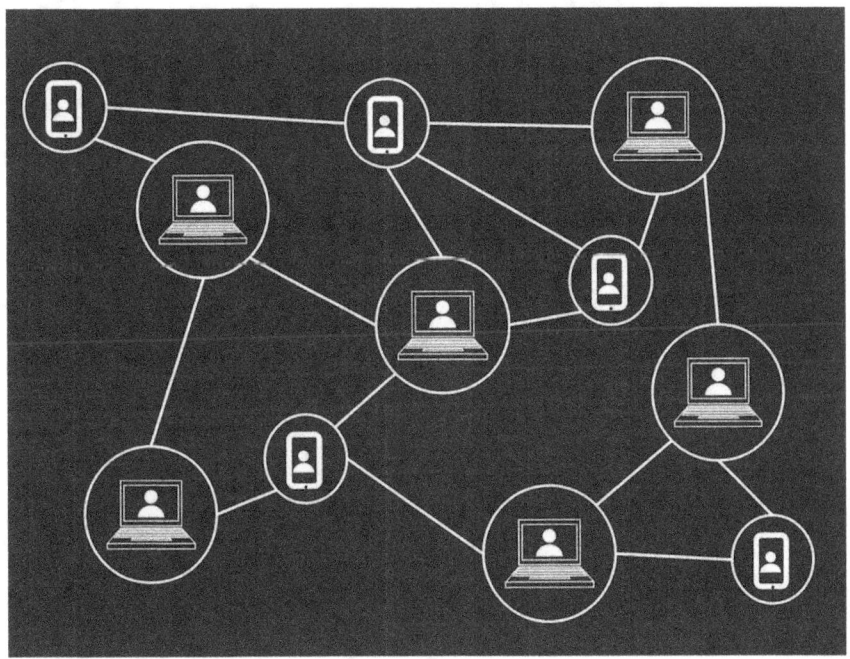

All transactions, however, do need to follow an agreed upon set of rules to be validated and completed. These rules are extremely complex and deeply embedded into everything on the Blockchain. Anyone who may manage to figure out how to change one block would have to subsequently change every other block on all the computers in the network to be successful, making tampering virtually impossible.

To better understand the Blockchain, one could think of it has a foundation that is used to transmit all forms of digital information. It is the network that gives support to all forms of cryptocurrencies. No matter what type of currency you are investing in, all transactions are recorded in the Blockchain.

Difference Between Cryptocurrency and Digital Currency

This is an important distinction that separates cryptocurrencies from other digital currencies, which have been around for many years. If you use an ATM card, a credit card, or a PayPal account you're already familiar with digital currencies. While cryptocurrencies are also digital currencies, it is the Blockchain that makes them different. The digital currency your bank uses, when your employer makes an automatic deposit into your bank account are currencies that have been recorded in a private ledger that is maintained on a centralized server. Cryptocurrencies are recorded in a public ledger maintained on the Blockchain.

Whether your interest is in Ethereum or in any other form of cryptocurrency, all transactions performed must be verified and added to the Blockchain.

Ethereum

To understand Ethereum, you must first understand its forerunner, Bitcoin, the first cryptocurrency in the world. Bitcoin was designed specifically for currency exchange so if you wanted to transfer funds to another person, make a purchase, or pay for services you could use Bitcoin in the same way as you could use traditional digital currency.

The difference lies in the verification process. Rather than having a middleman to access a centralized server and validate the data, all details are encrypted and dropped into a "mempool," where miners (people who prepare the blocks) pick it up and put it through a complex decoding process to validate it. Once validated, it is put into a block and added to the Blockchain.

The system worked well and allowed for peer-to-peer transactions without the need of an expensive financial institution to execute it. Bitcoin quickly gained popularity, and it wasn't long before it was being adopted all around the world, but it wasn't without flaws. In its early years, some complications and obstacles had to be overcome, but in time, it was clear that Bitcoin and Blockchain Technology was much more effective and less expensive than the traditional system.

In time, many programmers latched onto the concept and realized that the Blockchain Technology could be adapted to other aspects of the digital world that went beyond simply transferring currency.

Ethereum became the brainchild of one Russian-Canadian programmer by the name of Vitalik Buterin. After giving careful consideration to the problems with Bitcoin, he concluded that using the Blockchain strictly for currency was only tapping into a minute area of possibilities. As a result of his careful analysis, he created a whole new use for the

Blockchain, smart contracts.

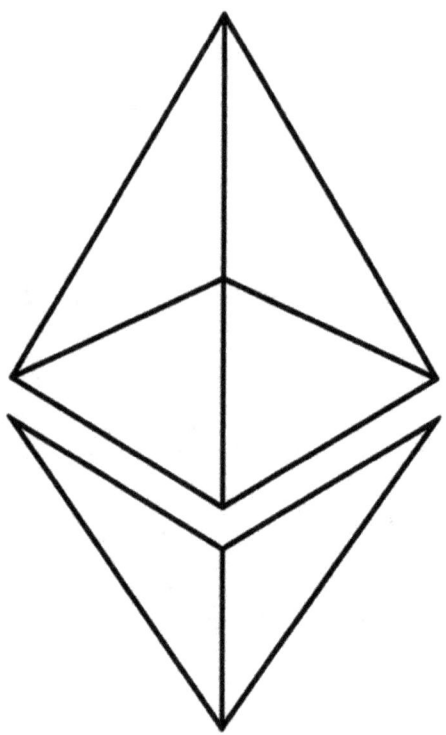

Buterin concluded that the Blockchain couldn't distinguish if

the digital data it received represented currency or not, so he formulated a way to store other types of information into the system as well and created a completely new type of Blockchain and called it Ethereum.

What made Ethereum's Blockchain different? While it was very similar in function to Bitcoin's Blockchain, there were some pretty distinct differences.

- It was faster, creating a new block every 15 seconds compared to Bitcoin's blocks being created every 10 minutes.

- It was better connected. The original developer of Bitcoin is still yet to be identified, but the creator of Ethereum is personally invested in the future of his coin.

- The creation of smart contracts allows Ethereum to go far beyond what Bitcoin could ever hope to achieve.

Their implementation allows two parties who do not know each other to create a self-executing agreement without third party involvement.

The main idea behind Ethereum was to add another level of coding to the encryption method already being used by Bitcoin. The concept behind this addition was that it opened up possibilities for actions that Bitcoin could never do.

Blocks on the Ethereum Blockchain are much more complex, but the complexity is what allows it to do so many things. So, how does this actually work? These added layers of coding are used to create something called Smart Contracts.

What are Smart Contracts?

Smart contracts are a digitized form of the same contracts we have been using for years. They were developed to remove another type of middleman, the lawyers, notaries, and brokers of businesses in the same way that Bitcoin removed the need for a bank. With a smart contract, you can create a self-executed program based on the specific parameters of an agreement between two parties without those specialists involved.

The extra layer of coding allows users to create pre-programmed contracts that will trigger certain actions as soon as agreed upon obligations have been met. Unlike Bitcoin, however, Ethereum cannot be used as a means of monetary currency. You can't use it to purchase a home or a car, but you can use Ethereum to create contracts for those types of purchases.

This is possible by means of something call Solidity, which is a computerized language used with smart contracts. To create this extra layer of coding, a system had to be developed that could take the terms of a contract and recreate it in a digitized form so it could be stored on the Blockchain.

Based on the terms the users would lay out in the contract, once certain actions were met (a payment for example) the system would automatically execute preset functions. There are many ways this has benefited the business world and Ethereum users.

- Smart contracts can allow voters to place their ballots entirely online without fear of the system being hacked or tampered with.

- Transfer of real estate property becomes easier with Ethereum contracts.

- Medical professionals can maintain patient records on the Blockchain with the assurance that only those authorized can have access to it.

No doubt there are many more ways that smart contracts will be used in the future. As more and more people realize its potential, it is poised to affect nearly every industry in the world.

The language also allows users to develop and create tokens so they can become their own central bank capable of issuing money in the form of a puzzle-based cryptocurrency of their own.

With that capability, users can create a crowdfunding campaign to raise funds for organizations without going through any centralized servers to monitor the funds. This can be done in complete anonymity beyond those that are actually involved in the action.

Using Solidity, users can prevent parties from interpreting the terms of an agreement in their own way, once the parameters are set, the system will automatically verify and enforce the contract based on the terms set out in the language without deviation.

Besides using these contracts with currencies, all sorts of businesses can make use of these agreements including agreements made when trading stocks, crowdfunding, voting, auctions, copyright protection, medical records, registries, insurance, lotteries, managing taxes, and so much more.

In addition to the smart contracts, the Ethereum Virtual Machine (EVM), a software program designed to allow anyone to run it regardless of the programming language they use, makes it possible to use the platform in thousands of an endless number of ways.

Because of all these added features, Ethereum is much more adaptable to all sorts of services so whether you want to issue a loan, cast a vote, transfer property, or almost anything else, it is most likely possible with Ethereum. This is one of the main reasons why more and more people are attracted to Ethereum. Not only is it adaptable to a wide variety of consumer needs, because of its decentralized platform it is virtually tamper-proof, but it also can't be censored, and is one of the safest means of conducting transactions to date.

What is Ether?

If you've been doing any research on Ethereum, you've probably already heard of Ether. When you invest in Ethereum, you're actually buying Ether, which can be considered to be the currency or the "money" that is used to pay for the transactions performed on the Ethereum network.

This means that technically, you are not going to be investing in Ethereum but in the Ether used to perform transactions on the network. You can probably liken it to the fuel that propels your car. Without fuel, your car will not operate, and without Ether, Ethereum will not function. So, when you invest your money in Ethereum, you will actually be buying Ether.

If you want to define the differences between Bitcoin and Ethereum even more clearly, you could think of Ethereum as an extension of Bitcoin. It picks up where its predecessor stops. But the differences lie not just in how it is used but in its technology. It is more than just a means of transferring currency, users can create their own programs to trade, or they may choose to create their own Initial Coin Offering to fund a new coin of their own.

Bottom line, the purpose of Ethereum is to put more power into the hands of its users giving them a means to develop their own decentralized applications that can apply more directly to their needs.

Chapter 2: Getting Set Up for Ethereum Investing

Before you can begin to invest in Ethereum, you need to have a few things in place. You cannot just walk into an Ethereum shop and submit an application for Ether (the fuel that makes Ethereum run) and walk out with some in your hand.

Ethereum, like all other cryptocurrencies, exists only in the digital world and so all of your investing tools need to also be digital. For that, you need to set up an Ethereum account. There are several steps you need to take to get started.

You Need a Wallet:

One of the first things you need to do is to set up your wallet. There are many wallets to choose from each having their own advantages and disadvantages. Ideally, you want a wallet that is user-friendly has a supportive development community and is compatible with your own computer system.

Your wallet is really just a computer software program that can connect to the network when you need to. When you download the software, it will come in a zip file you will need to open and launch on your computer. Once it is downloaded, it needs to connect to and sync with the Ethereum network. Finally, it is important to test the application, create a password, and store it in a secure location for further use.

The type of wallet you choose will depend on your specific needs. If you plan to do frequent trades, it is recommended that you have more than one wallet. Ideally, you want a cold wallet (one that is not connected to the Internet until you need it) to store the bulk of your currency and a hot wallet (one that you can quickly transfer funds in and out of) when you are ready to make a transaction.

While each wallet has its own security protocols in place, it is important to understand that those security measures are only as good as the care you take in protecting your keys from being used. Since the only way to access your funds is by use of your keys, it is up to you to take the extra precautions to ensure that those keys do not end up in the wrong hands.

Here is a list of characteristics you should look for in a good wallet:

- You should have complete control over what happens to your keys

- It should be easy to use

- There should be a well-defined support system.

- You have the ability to backup your wallet and restore it if something were to happen.

- It should be compatible with a number of computer systems

Mist: Mist is considered the official wallet for Ethereum users, but it is not the only one. The Mist wallet requires 9.5 MB of space on your computer or your external USB drive so make sure that your computer system has enough room to hold it. Once you download and launch it, you should first try to test it out before you actually start funding it with real cash. You can do this by accessing the "Test the Network" feature. When you are sure that there are no complications with syncing your wallet with your computer you can move on to the next step, setting up your account.

Set Up an Exchange Account

Next, you need to set up an exchange account. This is the where you will send and receive Ether when you begin making your transactions. Once your account is set up, you'll also have to be extra careful to ensure that it is secure. It will be password protected, but that will only be as safe as you are in making sure that no unauthorized person has access. This includes protecting your password by keeping it in a secure location, preferably in a place that cannot be accessed by the Internet. There is no such thing as a password retrieval set up on your account and so if it's lost so is the path to your money.

There are quite a few exchanges to choose from so it is important that you don't just pick the first one you find. There are a number of factors you want to take into consideration before you make a final decision.

- Find an exchange that allows you to buy Ether

- Make sure the location of the exchange is one that can meet your needs. Many exchanges are located in other countries, which means their governing laws may be different from what you are familiar with. Also, there is the possibility of dealing with a language barrier if for some reason you need customer support.

- Find out what security measures they have in place to protect your money. It is true that cryptocurrency is more secure than traditional currency but that it is not a guarantee that someone is not already taking measures to overcome the obstacles already in place. Your exchange should have some security measures in place to ensure that they are protected from cyber attacks, viruses, or malware.

- You also want to be aware of the many transaction fees that the exchange charges. Most people get very excited about making a profit but quickly forget to factor in the transaction fees when they finalize a deal. The result is that they could actually lose money if they're not careful so know what you will have to pay for each transaction before you set up an account.

coinbase

Some of the most trusted exchanges you might want to consider are Coinbase, Poloniex, Kraken, and Bitfinex. You will be required to provide identification proof to get set up. This is a precautionary measure to ensure that money launderers or anyone else who may perform illegal acts won't have access to their network.

Some exchanges do not require you to have an account to buy or sell Ether, but they are primarily used by those who have other forms of cryptocurrency that they want to exchange for Ether. While these can be quite convenient and offer a certain level of privacy, be extra careful on these sites as you never know who you're dealing with.

Fund Your Account

Next, you want to fund your account. Most exchanges will allow you to do this with a bank credit card, a debit card, or a bank transfer. The quicker option is with a credit or debit card as the funds reach your account almost instantly. However, if you're willing to wait a little bit to get into the game, many exchanges will offer you a higher deposit limit if you fund your account by bank transfer.

Now that your wallet and account are set up you are ready to begin trading. There are a lot of ways you can set up a transaction and more than a few investment strategies. In the following chapter, we'll cover some of the simpler investment and trading strategies to start with. As you gain more knowledge and experience in dealing with Ethereum, you can delve into more challenging projects, but if you're a newbie to this cryptoworld, we strongly recommend that you ease into it with a few simple buy and sell strategies to start with.

Chapter 3: Tips on Analyzing Ethereum

There is still one more thing you should do before you start actually trading. You need to determine when is the best time to get in or out of the market. This will require you to do some analyzing of different charts and graphs.

This can be a little scary for the newcomer. Looking at those charts can be overwhelming when you don't know what all those lines, colors, and bars actually mean. Of course, there are a lot of charts to look at, but we'll just talk about some of the most basic ones. As you master the fundamentals, you can then try your hand at some of the more detailed charts.

Because newcomers are often treading in unfamiliar territory, it is easy for them to take the easy way out and rely on the advice of experts. Go to any website that monitors cryptocurrency, and you'll hear experts voicing all sorts of opinions on when to buy and to sell. This may be good in theory, you assume like most of us, that these people know the market much better than you but the reality is that even experts can also make mistakes or may not be the best judge of performance. The end game they're looking for may not match your personal investment goals.

This is why listening to their views may be very educational, but it is also important for you to learn how to do the analysis yourself. After all, they do not have your same expectations for the investment you are making.

That said, there are two types of analysis you can apply when you're deciding when to get into the market or to get out: fundamental and technical.

Fundamental Analysis

Fundamental analysis involves a careful evaluation of the currency's financial health. Unlike with a stock, cryptocurrencies do not have any type of financial statements to study. This is because they are not corporations so you don't have a driver at the helm that is spearheading the way the coin will perform. What you do have, however, is a community that is backing its use.

Another reason fundamental analysis is not always easy is that most crypto coins are still too young to have a history long enough to tell a story. Ethereum was only introduced into the cryptoworld in 2014, so it is barely three years in the making.

Therefore it is important that before you begin to analyze Ethereum that you understand your approach has to be different from that of the stock exchange. You will have to do additional research to assess the potential and the right time to enter the market. Once you understand Ethereum's fundamentals, you will be able to formulate your own opinions and make your own predictions free from the advice you get from strangers no matter how knowledgeable they might be.

Where to Look: It starts with looking at the right resources. There are several places you could go. We already talked about listening to experts who voice their opinion but to develop your own sense of Ether's movements you need to go directly to the source.

- You can start by looking at Ether's white paper. This is a detailed outline of the purpose and the mechanics of the coin. Always go to the white paper before you spend your first dime.

- Check the slack channel where the development team interacts with the community of Ether users. This is where you can ask your questions and get clarification of points you don't fully understand in the white paper.

- Finally, keep up with the community forums to help you understand what is going on with Ether and how it could affect its price movements. There will always be a wide variety of people speaking on the platform so the discussions may open up your mind to perspectives you haven't even considered.

What to Look for: Your goal is to understand what events or actions can cause the price to move up or down. To that end, there are several questions you should consider getting answers to.

GitHub

- How active is the development?

In most cases, you will find the activity profile on the Github. It will tell you what are the plans for the project and what new features are scheduled to be implemented. This will give you a good picture of what the development team has in store for the future.

- Is the development team actively interacting with the community?

The more the development team engages with the community, the better its chances of growing in the future. Since it is the community that propels the coin forward, community involvement is crucial to the future of the coin.

- Characteristics of the coin

This could include the current market cap and its distribution.

It can be really fun to measure Ether against other forms of investments and see its growth and think that it has a long a prosperous future. However, one should never forget that even though Ethereum currently has all the elements of a solid investment, it is still very much in its infancy stage and careful evaluation on a regular basis is necessary to lower your amount of risk exposure.

Keep in mind that Ethereum's continued success lies in whether or not they can continue to produce quality apps and new ideas to keep them ahead of the pack.

Technical Analysis

Performing a technical analysis is a little more detailed than a fundamental analysis. This is where you have to begin a careful examination of all those charts and graphs you're finding online. Common sense dictates that the way to make a profit is by buying low and selling high but when you see a price steadily dropping, how do you know when it has reached its lowest point, and it's time to buy or how can you tell that a price has reached its pinnacle and is about to fall again.

These questions are the reason you perform a technical analysis before you buy. Your biggest question you want to be answered is "when" to get in and get out. A good technical analysis will give you a good picture of the historic pricing trends. Once you understand these trends, it will be easier to predict the direction the price is most likely to move.

The easiest trends to spot are the uptrends and the downtrends. You can identify downtrends by a series of highs that are gradually lowering over a period of time. Uptrends are when the highs are gradually getting higher over time. We all know that prices do not flow in a straight vertical path; they zigzag across the chart going up and down throughout any given time frame, but when you study the chart over a period of time, the prevailing direction of the price can be easily identified.

Support and Resistance: Support and resistance levels appear when you see a large number large number of buyers or sellers appearing around the same time. When you see this type of trend, it is a good time to buy as the more buyers entering the market will push the price up to the point of resistance where it can't go any higher.

Resistance levels is just the opposite where you can see a large number of sellers exiting the market to the point where it can't go any lower. When you see resistance points in the price trend, it is a good time to sell.

As you become more familiar with the patterns that emerge on these charts and graphs, you will naturally develop an intuition about which direction the prices will go. Of course, you can't buy and sell every time you see these patterns appear, but if you analyze them and develop an infinity for recognizing the ebbs and flows of the charts, you'll be able to pinpoint the best time to enter and exit the market to capitalize on your profits.

By following just a few guidelines, the potential for profitability will increase.

Step 1: Determine your entry and exit points based on your analysis

Step 2: Decide on an investment strategy based on the patterns you identify.

Step 3: Execute the strategy.

Step 4: Determine your stop/loss points and stick to them.

While this may seem a little complicated, it is really pretty basic. Like all things that may be unfamiliar to you, it just takes getting to know them to see a positive result. The good news is that you don't have to be correct all the time to see a profit so if you see the price drop from time to time after you make your investment, there is little reason to stress. Things change quickly with cryptocurrency, and it is a highly volatile market, even with the more stable coins like Ethereum. Just stay the course, and it will usually pay off in the end.

Chapter 4: Investment Strategies

Now that you're all set up with your account, you have your wallet, and you've done your research, you're now ready to get into the market. One of the first things you will do is to get some Ether. If you're new to the market, then the logical conclusion is that you must buy it, but there are other ways you can obtain the Ether to fill your wallet.

If you are one of those who have a bit of computer programming skills and you know your way around hard drives, GPUs, and ASICs, then you could also try your hand at mining it, but clearly, that is not for everyone. The role of the miner is to verify transactions and create a block to add to the Blockchain.

However, mining can be a bit complicated; trying to make sense of the consensus algorithms, investing the amount of time and money required for the equipment and the energy it needs to run it can put the prospect out of reach for many.

Many believe it is worth the risk. When you consider that an investor must spend a lot of time researching to predict the movements of the market, the return on investment can be a lot more promising. When mining, you compete with the other miners to be the first to solve a particular block; it could be days, weeks, or even months before you could be the first in line. In the meantime, you are paying out quite a bit of money in energy trying to get to that day. Those who choose to outright invest or trade for their earnings feel they have more control over their ability to make money. Even with better prospects for earning money, investing is not the best choice for everyone. Whether it is the right path for you depends on you as a person and how much risk you are willing to take. To determine that, it is wise to learn why so many others have chosen to invest in Ethereum.

The fact that Ethereum has a growing popularity for investors and users alike tells us that there is a strong possibility that profits will remain in its future for quite some time. With the cost of Bitcoin, soaring out of reach for many, it is only natural that new investor's eyes will fall to the number two coin.

No doubt, you will soon find there are many ways to acquire Ether.

There are even websites that will give it away like radio stations that offer prizes for call-ins and answering questions and such. But for the sake of this book, we'll restrict our comments to investment strategies that have proven effective in the past.

The strategy that you choose will depend on your goals, your time frame, and your risk tolerance so there is no one way to get in or out of Ethereum, you just need to choose the strategy that works best for your personal circumstances.

Buy and Hold

This strategy simply means that you obtain your Ether and hold onto it for an extended period of time. Those who employ this strategy usually plan to store their Ether for a year or longer. The idea behind it is simple; while the price will often fluctuate over time, going up and down frequently, the general trend is in the upward direction. Investors who apply this strategy already have an endgame in mind. They are not just waiting until it reaches a price that they like, but they have already set their sights on a specific goal. This could be a certain price point, but it doesn't have to be, sometimes they are looking for the market cap to reach a certain level, or they want the volume to reach a certain point. Whatever their set goal is, they are determined not to sell until it reaches that point. The goals you set will be decided after you've done your analysis and predicted the direction it will go.

No doubt, this is probably the easiest ways to invest in Ethereum, but it is not always the cheapest. You simply buy and wait until your goals are met and then sell. For this strategy to be successful, you need to think it through before you buy. By doing this, you can ensure that your emotions won't get involved and cause you to make a knee-jerk reaction that could actually restrict your profit potential.

The buy and hold strategy is perfect for anyone that doesn't have the desire, time or the experience needed to dedicate to monitoring charts all the time. This does not mean that you don't have to watch the charts, but you won't have to be continuously reviewing them.

Selling Short

The selling short strategy is a bit more difficult to master than the buy and hold. This is for those who want to get in and out of the market quickly without dedicating a long period of time. While the buy and hold strategy is extended to a year or more, selling short could be anything under a year. You might get in the market one minute, and if the price of Ether rises to your target the next day, you can pull out taking your profits with you. Sometimes you could even sell off your Ether within just a few minutes of purchasing.

The challenge involved in making this strategy a success depends on how much research work you dedicate to it. You really need to be familiar with the price movements and understand the trends to earn a profit this way.

The ideal strategist is very adept at taking advantage of the natural price fluctuations of the market, and they have to time their entrance and exit the market at the precise time.

Selling short is a high-stress form of investment as every second counts. The investor who does best is less likely to react emotionally to the constant market fluctuations and can resist the temptation to react impulsively. They must rely more on their analytic skills rather than on the movement of prices. Those that can develop them are quite likely to get some pretty high returns in a very short amount of time.

It is extremely important that there is a definite plan of action in place before you get into the market. You need to have a decision on when to sell and why and when to buy to make a clear profit. If you would like to give short selling a try ask yourself these questions:

- When do I want to sell

- What percentage of return will I set as my target

- How much of a hit will I be able to take

- Is this the only way I can get this type of return

Being able to answer these types of questions honestly can reveal a great deal about yourself as an investor. It will help you to see what you really hope to get out of your strategy and it gives you a structure for planning your investments in the future.

Those who are the most successful at short selling are those who have had the time to hone in on their analytic skills.

Most beginners struggle with this strategy so test the waters first by investing in small amounts of Ether before you attempt to go at it full on. While you won't make nearly as much money as you would with a larger investment, you cut your risk levels down considerably until you get the hang of it.

Dollar Cost Averaging

Investing can be an expensive venture and most people do not have the funds on hand to go full on with their first venture. In cases such as those, they usually have two options; first, they can borrow the money to put into their investment choices, which is great if they can turn a profit on the venture, and the second choice is something called dollar cost averaging.

Dollar cost averaging is the practice of putting small amounts of money into the investment on a regular basis. The idea behind it is that during some periods the cost of the coin will be higher than other times, but overall the price of the coins will average out so you won't be paying the highest prices nor will you be paying the lowest.

Analysts say that dollar cost averaging is the perfect way to lower the impact of price volatility because you're never purchasing large sums of currency at a single time.

The strategy is very simple:

- Determine the total amount of money you would like to invest

- Divide that amount out over equal time periods (this could be weekly, monthly, quarterly, etc.)

- During each time period, purchase small amounts of Ether until you have the total number of coins you want to acquire or you have exhausted all of your scheduled time periods.

There are many good reasons why you would want to use this strategy for investing. It not only gives you a hedge against losses from the constant price movements or major declines in price but it increases your odds of turning a profit without having to shell out a lot of cash in the process.

This is not to say that there are no flaws in this system. Every strategy has its own downsides, and it is not very effective with every type of cryptocurrency. In fact, it is the perfect mechanism for currencies that have a pretty steady and predictable pattern of price movements with only a temporary drop in price like Ethereum. This way, if you do purchase some currency at a higher price during one pay period, you can easily make up for it at the next one.

The advantages are easy to see. Investing in this manner, you can capitalize on the fluctuations of the market. The periods where the price is lower will allow you to purchase more coins than when the price is higher because you will be investing the exact same amount each period.

While you will still have to do your analysis, you won't be as concerned with following every single movement in the market. And as statistics often show, the market will have frequent highs and lows in prices. However, the general trend for tried and proven currencies like Ethereum is a price that is continuously on the rise.

Still, you don't want to assume that it is all peaches and cream either. Negative market trends do happen from time to time, and even if you think it is better to ride out a major downtrend, you always need to be ready to respond when things don't recover as expected. It wouldn't be smart to continue to ride a wave that is destined to cause you to lose all your money in hopes that things will turn around. It's a great strategy as long as you are continuing to get the returns you're hoping for.

Knowing When to Get in the Market

We have already touched on this subject a little bit in the last chapter, but it bears repeating. Most new investors are more concerned about when to get out of the market, but you should dedicate a good amount of time to when to get in as well.

The inexperienced investor sees the price rising rapidly, and his first impulse is to get in and ride the wave to the top. That works well if you get in at the beginning of the wave but what should you do if the wave has been escalating for a while?

Inevitably, the price will reach a point where it will have to fall again; this is the natural movement of the market. Even successful coins like Ethereum will see a downtrend after a meteoric rise, so it is important to exercise patience and wait for the downtrend. Otherwise, you might find yourself getting in at a high price only to see it plummet to the floor in a matter of days taking all your money down with it.

Ideally, you're looking for a point when the price is no longer rising or when it is on a decline. As a general rule of thumb, it is important to wait until the price has reached some level of stability before you decide to buy in. This way, your chances of earning a bigger profit are much higher than if you just jump in without a plan.

There is no right or wrong way to invest in Ethereum. Whether you want to buy, sell, or trade, you need to know yourself first. What is your investment style? What is your tolerance for risk? What do you hope to get? Once you can identify the kind of investor you are, it will be much easier for you to determine which strategy will work the best for your investment plan. Just keep in mind that no matter what the market is doing, it is never a good idea to rush your decision when it comes to any type of cryptocurrency. The natural volatility of the market is enough to take your breath away at times so always have a plan and know what you hope to get out of it and you increase your chances of producing positive returns and profits in your future.

Chapter 5: Ethereum Trading

Many newcomers often assume that investing and trading are the same thing. While there are some definite similarities between the two, there are some marked differences as well. The investor is actually interested in "owning" the currency they obtain. They are in the practice of buying and selling. This is the only way they can realize the earnings they set out to achieve.

Traders, on the other hand, never own their currency and are more interested in speculating on the price movements. Because they never take possession of the currency, they do not need to pay out the full value of the currency when they place a trade but only a small percentage.

Traders do not use the same type of trading account as an investor but must set up a special account with the exchange or a broker. This way they gain a huge amount of exposure to the market without having to pay a lot of cash.

While this is an excellent way to make a lot of money in a short period of time, it does not come without its own set of risks. If the prices move as you expect them to, then the rewards are great, but if the price moves against you, it exposes you to huge losses as well. You will have to cover those losses at some point.

So, to be successful as a trader, there are some pretty important guidelines you should follow. Strategies used in the previous chapter on investment can be applied to trading but with much more care. If you want to try your hand at trading here are some additional points you must keep in mind to protect your assets and boost your chances of earning a profit.

Pay Careful Attention to Market Volatility

Even more stable coins like Bitcoin and Ethereum will see extreme price fluctuations, which can be very tempting to take advantage of. It can be a really crazy roller coaster ride, so you might have the impulse to jump ahead of the market and not do your homework, which could be disastrous for the trader.

Always proceed with caution. Traders need to know more than that there is a hike or a drop in prices. If you can learn to keep your head when things get crazy, then you'll be that much better off. While there are always risks, you need to understand exactly what you have at stake when you initiate a trade. A major drop in price when you were anticipating a spike could wipe out your entire investment and some in a very short amount of time.

One thing that most people do not like to think about is the risk that could result from a problem in the software. Source code bugs could infiltrate the system and cause problems that could wipe out your investment. While this is not likely to happen with Ethereum, keep in mind that there are new codes and Dapps (decentralized applications) being added to the system all the time. There is always a risk of a new bug slipping into the system causing problems.

While we are not saying that these are things that will happen, they are definitely risks that you must keep foremost in your mind when you start trading. There is nothing more risky to a trader than not knowing the risks.

However, if you are prepared to accept the negatives that may come along, let's talk about a few trading strategies you might want to try.

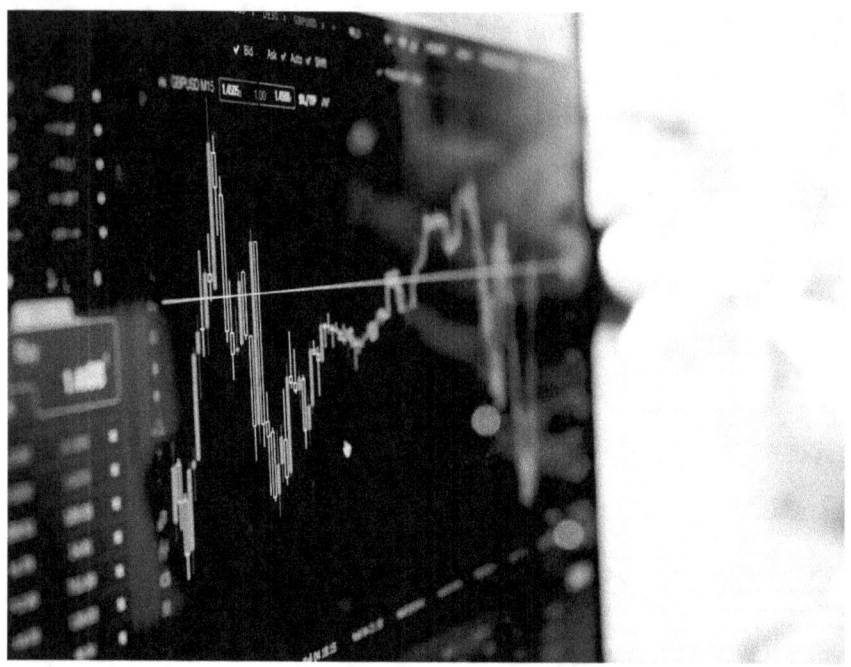

Day Trading

If you're one of those people who is looking for a fast-paced environment, then you'll love day trading. It is very similar to the selling short strategy we spoke about in the last chapter but with much more intensity. The concept is simple, you buy and sell on the same day. No matter what the market is doing, you exit the market before you close your eyes to go to sleep that night and never leave your money in overnight.

The benefits of day trading are obvious. Rewards are immediate. Imagine turning a profit in a matter of hours or even minutes rather than waiting for weeks or months to see the results. You never have to worry about what the market will do when you go to sleep and if your investment will keep until the market opens the next morning.

But there is a very ugly side to day trading as well. You have to be a pretty strong and resourceful person to withstand the pressures of this type of fast-paced trading. There is no break when you're day trading, the difference between making a fortune and losing everything can happen in a matter of seconds. Not everyone is cut out for the intensity of this type of trade, and it can really put a lot of stress on your heart if you're not ready.

Margin Trading

Margin trading is probably the riskiest of all types of profit-making ventures. When you market trade, you are using someone else's money and not your own. Therefore the risk of loss is even more frightening. If you fail and your market predictions are off, you lose someone else's money, and you may find yourself having losing everything you've put in as well, and getting absolutely nothing in return.

Traders usually borrow the money for the transactions from the exchange and leave a deposit that is equivalent to a percentage of the amount borrowed as security. If their predictions are correct, then both the trader and the exchange can earn huge profits, but if their predictions are wrong, the responsibility lies on the shoulders of the trader.

Let's see how this works. Imagine that you have on hand (your own personal money) $10,000 to trade. You can approach the exchange and ask for a 1:4 leverage, which would allow you to trade $40,000. You will put up your $10,000, and the exchange would cover the other $30,000.

If the price of Ether begins to rise, the total profit also rises but, if it begins to fall, your losses also increase. Your percentage of the total investment is 25% so if your losses fall below that 25% mark, you will lose all of your money. If the price falls below that 25% mark, the exchange will close out your position leaving you without the option to wait for the price to recover. In other words, your $10,000 stake will serve as collateral against your loss.

This example goes to show just how risky such a venture can be and considering the volatility of the market, anything can happen even under the best of circumstances. Of course, you don't need to follow the 1:4 trade, you could choose to invest the 1:3 or 1:2, which could increase your odds considerably.

Just keep in mind that the higher the leverage, the higher your risk.

You also need to keep in mind that there will be additional interest to be paid on the borrowed money, which can amount to quite a bit. Many exchanges charge this interest rate on a daily basis. That is one reason why margin traders are quick to get in and out of the market because the fees for staying in a trade for too long can really begin to add up and undoubtedly will take all of your profits with it.

The best advice for traders is to...

- Only trade when the value of Ether has experienced a major drop.

- Only close a position if you have managed to earn between 20 and 50% profit

- Don't fail to factor in the commission fees and interest.

Long-Term Trading

There is also a form of long-term trading, which is best suited for those who do not have eight hours a day to sit in front of the computer. They may prefer to trade on a set day of the week rather than make trades on a daily basis. If you choose long-term trading, you should...

- Choose the same day to trade every week

- Monitor the news throughout the week, so you have an idea of the what is happening to the currency before you trade

If you follow these very basic guidelines, your chances of effective trading could yield you a nice profit.

As a trader, the key to your success is diligent research and self-control. Being able to hold back when you're not sure and jump in when you are is not as easy as it sounds. In addition, the person who can withstand fast-paced pressure is very important. If you're the kind of person that jumps at every change, worries about every movement then trading is probably not right for you. But if you can handle intense pressure and the responsibility of handling someone else's money then you are in for a wild ride if you decide to be a trader.

Chapter 6: Ways to Invest in Ethereum

So far, we've managed to discuss what to do and when to do it, but there is one other point we must address before we turn you lose into the world of Ethereum. You need to know exactly how to buy, sell, and trade on the exchange.

You already know the initial steps to set up your wallet and to open an account on the exchange. As an investor, buying Ether is as simple as going to the buy/sell button on your account dashboard and placing an order. However whether you're buying, selling, or trading there is a lot more you can do to make sure you have covered all your bases.

When you want to open or close your position on the exchange, you must place an order. There are several different types of orders you can place depending on what you want to accomplish.

Pending Orders: are orders for actions you want to take in the future. A limit order is an order to sell or buy when the price reaches a certain point. A market order is an order to buy or sell as soon as it is entered. When you place a market order, you set an ask price, and the exchange will sell your Ether at the price that is closest to your ask price.

Stop Orders: are those orders set to buy or sell if the price goes beyond a particular point. So, for example, if you set your stop at $500 then once the price exceeds that amount, your stop order is automatically converted to a market order, and your Ether will be bought or sold at a price closest to your order price.

Stop-Limit Orders: is a combination of a pending order and a stop order. You must set two price points, the first one starts a specific action and the second one stops the action.

GTC Orders: are those that indicate you want the action to continue until you decide to cancel it. (Good Till Canceled)

There are many ways you can invest in Ethereum as well as many ways to place orders. Don't be afraid to utilize these tools, they will help you to find success and prevent you from losing everything when things turn south. Ethereum has a very promising future, and it is expected to continue to grow in the coming years, but that does not mean it is without risk.

By learning how to use the orders set up on your exchange, you can protect yourself to some degree from excessive losses but at the same time open up the door to untold profits at every turn.

Conclusion

Thank you for making it through to the end of this book, let's hope it was informative and able to provide you with all of the tools you need to achieve your goals whatever they may be.

As you can see, there is a lot more to learn about investing and trading in Ether. It all may sound very complicated, but once you get the hang of it, you'll be able to invest or trade with confidence. If you haven't already realized, investing in cryptocurrency is not just about the money. It requires a very specific mindset to be successful. It is not for everyone but if you are drawn to it, compelled by it, and inspired, this just may be your calling.

If you're ready to test it out, here are just a few final notes that could put you on the right path to success.

- Keep your head: Even if the price is rising, don't stay in the game too long. Inevitably, it will come down and take your profits with you.

- Don't rush: Patience is the key to everything. Waiting for the right time to buy is just as crucial as getting out at the right time. Patience can also keep you from panicking and making knee-jerk reactions to a naturally volatile market.

- Consider how many people are in the market with you: Many people fail to realize that the number of people buying and selling at the same time can give a false reading to the prices. Know who you're playing ball with, and you are less likely to be fooled.

Following these guidelines are enough to help you get started but if you're in this game for the long haul, don't stop here.

The more familiar you are with Ethereum and its movements, the better your chances of making a good profit when the time comes.

Finally, if you found this book useful in any way, a review on Amazon is always appreciated!